Ella the
Elephant

by Jan Latta

Reading consultant: Susan Nations, M.Ed., author/literacy coach/consultant in literacy development

Science and curriculum consultant: Debra Voege, M.A., science and math curriculum resource teacher

GARETH**STEVENS**
GS
PUBLISHING
A Member of the WRC Media Family of Companies

Hello! My name is Ella, and I am an elephant. I live in Africa with my family. We are the biggest **mammals** on land. Our **ancestors** lived on Earth about fifty million years ago.

At his shoulders, my father is 11 feet (3.5 meters) tall.
He weighs 11,910 pounds (5,400 kilograms). My mother
weighs 7,060 pounds (3,200 kg). My brother is so small
that he can stand under our mother's belly.

Our **tusks** are made of **ivory**. They can grow up to 10 feet (3 m) long!

Baby elephants are called calves. When we are born, we weigh about 220 pounds (100 kg). We drink our mother's milk for two years. We start eating grass when we are three months old. Our mother teaches us the best places to find food.

We find lots of grass in open areas of land. Sometimes, the Sun gets too hot for me. Then I stand under my mother to keep cool.

Our family is part of a **herd** of elephants.
The oldest mother is called the **matriarch**.
Every day, she guides our group to food
and water.

We go to the river to drink. I use my trunk to suck up water. I pull the water halfway into my trunk, like a straw. Then I put my trunk in my mouth and squirt the water down my throat. My father can drink up to 224 quarts (212 liters) of water in just five minutes!

Sometimes it is hard to get
in the water. A friendly push
can help!

I love to play and splash in the water. I can swim
underwater, using my trunk as a **snorkel**. Then
it is fun to roll in the mud with my brother.

We dust ourselves with dirt to protect our skin from flies and other insects that bite. Then we scratch ourselves against a rock.

Elephants are **herbivores**. We eat about 287 pounds (130 kg) of plants each day. We use our tusks to strip the tasty bark from trees. We loosen grass and roots with our feet. Our trunks help us reach fruit and leaves.

I walk on my toes. I have five toenails on each front foot and three on each of my back feet.

The bottoms of my feet are padded. Even though I am big, I can walk very quietly. I follow my family, and we walk in a single file line.

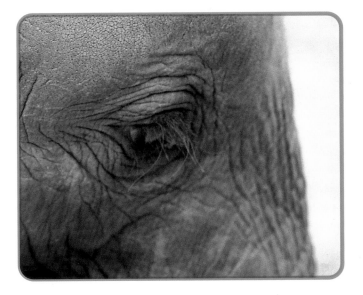

Very long eyelashes protect my eyes.

I have good hearing. I can flap my ears to keep cool.

My trunk is very strong and **flexible**. It has more than 150,000 muscles. I can use it as an arm, nose, or hand. It can pick up a tiny berry, but it is strong enough to break tree branches. I test my food with my tongue before I eat it.

Elephants use our trunks to greet each other. We can make a lot of noise by **trumpeting**, screeching, and bellowing. Sometimes we make low rumbles that humans cannot hear. Other elephants can hear us up to 5 miles (8 kilometers) away.

Our trunks can grow up to 10 feet (3 m). They can weigh up to 441 pounds (200 kg).

If our trunks feel heavy, we rest them on our tusks.

Can you see the difference between the African elephant above and the Asian elephant below?

I am an African elephant like my dad. Our ears are bigger than Asian elephants' ears. I will grow larger than my Asian cousins. Asian elephants are part of my wild animal family.

Elephant Facts

Did You Know?

- Elephants live in many kinds of places. They live in grassy areas or in forests. They also live in mountains and deserts.

- Elephants do not eat any meat. They only eat plants.

- An elephant grows six sets of teeth in its lifetime. It can only grow one set of tusks.

- Elephants are very smart. They have big brains and good memories.

- The elephant is related to the sea cow. Manatees and dugongs are two types of sea cow. Sea cows live in water and eat sea grass.

- The tip of an elephant's trunk has a very good sense of touch.

- Some elephants live to be seventy years old!

- Elephants sleep twice a day for about forty minutes. They sleep at noon while standing in the shade. They also sleep at midnight. Sometimes they snore!

- Father elephants are called bulls, and mothers are called cows.

- Pregnant elephants give birth after eighteen to twenty-two months.

- Elephant families stay close together. They like to touch each other with their trunks. They also rub their bodies and heads together. Family members look after calves.

- For more than three thousand years, people have worked with elephants. The ancient Greeks used them in their army.

- White elephants are sacred in India. People take very good care of them. They also do not make white elephants do any work.

- Elephant tusks are made of ivory. Sometimes people kill elephants for their ivory tusks. They make the ivory into statues and other pieces of art. Killing elephants is against the law.

Map — Where Elephants Live

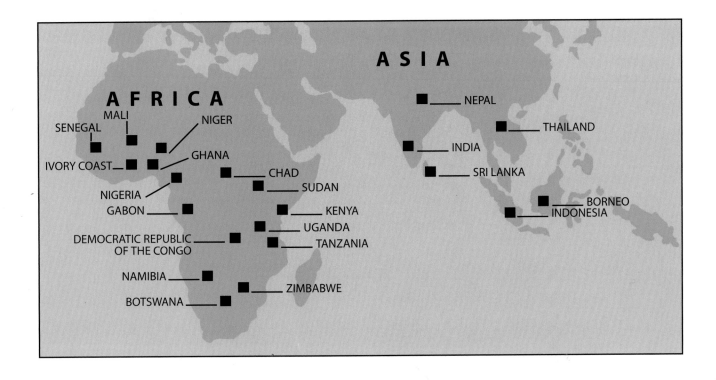

Glossary

ancestors — relatives that lived long before one's parents were born

flexible — easy to bend

herbivores — animals that eat only plants

herd — a large group of animals that are all the same kind

ivory — a hard, white material

mammals — animals that are covered with hair and give birth to babies that feed on milk

matriarch — the oldest mother in a family and often the head of the family

snorkel — a long tube used for breathing air while underwater

trumpeting — blowing to make a high-pitched noise that sounds like a trumpet

tusks — long white teeth that look like horns

More Information

Books

African Elephants Up Close. Zoom in on Animals! (series). Carmen Bredeson (Enslow Elementary)

Elephant. Watch Me Grow (series). DK Publishing (DK Children)

Little Elephants. Born to Be Wild (series). Anne Jonas (Gareth Stevens Publishing)

Web Sites

Kids' Planet
www.kidsplanet.org/factsheets/elephant.html
Find fast facts about elephants.

National Geographic for Kids: Elephants
www.nationalgeographic.com/kids/creature_feature/0103/elephants.html
Send a post card, watch a video, hear fun facts about elephants, and more.

Publisher's note to educators and parents: Our editors have carefully reviewed these Web sites to ensure that they are suitable for children. Many Web sites change frequently, however, and we cannot guarantee that a site's future contents will continue to meet our high standards of quality and educational value. Be advised that children should be closely supervised whenever they access the Internet.

Please visit our Web site at: www.garethstevens.com
For a free color catalog describing Gareth Stevens Publishing's list of high-quality books and multimedia programs, call 1-800-542-2595 (USA) or 1-800-387-3178 (Canada). Gareth Stevens Publishing's fax: (414) 332-3567.

Library of Congress Cataloging-in-Publication Data

Latta, Jan.
   Ella the elephant / by Jan Latta. — North American ed.
     p. cm. — (Wild animal families)
   Includes bibliographical references.
   ISBN-13: 978-0-8368-7768-7 (lib. bdg.)
   ISBN-13: 978-0-8368-7775-5 (softcover)
   1. Elephants—Juvenile literature. I. Title.
   QL737.P98L27   2007
   599.67—dc22   2006032121

This North American edition first published in 2007 by
Gareth Stevens Publishing
A Member of the WRC Media Family of Companies
330 West Olive Street, Suite 100
Milwaukee, WI 53212 USA

This U.S. edition copyright © 2007 by Gareth Stevens, Inc.
Original edition and photographs copyright © 2005 by Jan Latta.
First produced as *Adventures with Elle the Elephant* by
TRUE TO LIFE BOOKS, 12b Gibson Street, Bronte, NSW 2024 Australia

Acknowledgements: The author thanks Karl Ammann who generously allowed reproduction of his photographs on pages 12, 13 (bottom), and 18 (bottom). And thanks to Letaloi, the guide from Tortilis Camp in Amboseli, who gave her access to the elephants.

Project editor: Jan Latta
Design: Jan Latta

Gareth Stevens editorial direction: Valerie J. Weber
Gareth Stevens editor: Tea Benduhn
Gareth Stevens art direction: Tammy West
Gareth Stevens Graphic designer: Scott Krall
Gareth Stevens production: Jessica Yanke and Robert Kraus

Printed in Canada

1 2 3 4 5 6 7 8 9 10 10 09 08 07 06